Escalante

Gregory McNamee, SERIES EDITOR

BOOKS IN THE SERIES Desert Places

Escalante

The Best Kind of Nothing

TEXT BY Brooke Williams

PHOTOGRAPHS BY Chris Noble

The University of Arizona Press   Tucson

The University of Arizona Press
Text © 2006 Brooke Williams
Photographs © 2006 Chris Noble
All rights reserved
This book is printed on acid-free, archival-quality paper.
Manufactured in the United States of America

11 10 09 08 07 06   6 5 4 3 2 1

Library of Congress Cataloging-in-Publication Data appear on
the last printed page of this book.

Frontispiece: Escalante River bend

contents

CONTENTS

viii

photographs

PHOTOGRAPHS

X

Escalante

introduction

On a French map of the United States made in 1860, the area now known as the Colorado Plateau is labeled "Pays peu connu," which translates to "little-known country." While most of the map is detailed and dotted with the names of American cities and towns, this little-known country is white, blank, void. It is possible that a young French student using this map to learn world geography might have inquired about that blank white hole in America and been told, "There is nothing there," been led to believe that because this part of the world contains no lines marking political boundaries, no signs of civilizations, and no rivers or significant water bodies, that it is empty or dead. That because this part of the world was unknown to French mapmakers of the time; it simply did not exist.

Today, much of the Colorado Plateau is still relatively unknown and considered by many to be America's wild heart. For me, the core of that wild heart, the *heart* of the heart, is the region known as the Escalante.

Although I was not born in Utah, I've lived here my entire life, during half of which I've been making trips to the Escalante. I visited there first as a hiker and backpacker, lured into the deep canyons that time and wild weather has cut through this little-known country, by the same forces that have always pulled explorers to every end of the earth. Then during those early years, discussing whether the greater good of the Escalante is oil and cows or wildness, I went to work. First, I worked on issues aimed at protecting the beauty and diversity of that area I had loved since the first time I set foot there. Then, as a consultant, I worked at exploring ways to demonstrate that protecting wilderness might actually contribute to community wellbeing. Lately, I spend as much time inside—in meetings and discussions, arguments and strategic planning sessions—as I spend outside walking. It's a difficult balance to maintain.

"There is nothing out there." I have heard politicians say this while wondering why anyone would want to save that country. I have heard oil company executives say it, amazed that anyone would oppose the exploration and drilling of such absence. I have heard tourists using it as an excuse to drive directly to Capitol Reef and then on to Arches, as they peer over a

Hoodoos and gathering storm

road map while sitting in the Golden Loop Café on Main Street in the town of Escalante, waiting for their grilled cheese sandwiches.

And I have heard myself saying it, when asked why I would want to spend a precious week wandering the region's plateaus and canyon bottoms. There is nothing out there. To me, this is the best kind of Nothing.

OBVIOUSLY, there are varying ideas about *Nothing*.

To me, "nothing" has nothing to do with a void to be filled by the slightest external pressure. Nothing refers to "no-thing" and is the opposite of things, which have taken over our modern lives. It is obvious to me that any Nothing that has not given into things is a great and powerful force. Here, Nothing is not absence, but presence. Nothing is like silence, which in its true form is not soundless at all, but a deep pulsing that is not only heard but also felt. Nothing is like strong and powerful darkness, which can repel light and even absorb it. Our modern world has done its best to destroy Nothing and Silence and Darkness, and what remains of those three elements has become a force pressing us, pressure like water against which one can stand and be supported, a blessed fuel that enters through our eyes, through our ears, and through the pores in our skin.

The Escalante region is unique for many reasons, most of which are mentioned in the plan that justifies turning the area into a national monument: "The Monument was created to protect a spectacular array of historic, biological, geological, paleontological, and archaeological objects." The plan is III pages long, and I have read most of it. President Clinton's proclamation mentions everything from petrified wood, to biogeochemical cycles, to mammals of the Cenomanian and Santonian ages, but nothing about Nothing, Silence, and Darkness.

Perhaps we've been led to believe that modernity made it our task to overcome these things, and we've been very successful. And perhaps we're unwilling to acknowledge that there is a place within the United States where Nothing, Silence, and Darkness continue to thrive, and therefore we ignore them and pretend they don't exist.

Perhaps it was the combined energy of Nothing, Silence, and Darkness that can be blamed for what must be a mysterious force field pushing out from the middle of this region, deflecting all white men from entering, beginning with the Spanish priests Silvestre Velez de Escalante and Francisco Atanasio Dominguez and ending with the American explorer John Wesley Powell, during that hundred-year period when the entire West was being discovered, explored, and mapped. The entire West *but* the Escalante. It wasn't until 1872 that the first white man stood in the Escalante River drainage and actually knew where he was.

Today, the name Escalante is attached to a river, a town, a desert, an entire region, and now a national monument. At first it is easy to surmise that Escalante and his partner Dominguez visited the area in 1776 during a journey that may have been one of the most difficult ever made. They were looking for a route from Santa Fe, New Mexico, to Monterey, California, where Spanish missions had been established as early as 1580. Although early stories suggest that this ragged expedition, fueled by piñon, prickly pear,

Canyon cottonwood

and prayer, wandered into the Escalante Valley, Escalante's detailed journals make no mention of it. And history credits this expedition with discovering every major tributary of the Colorado River *except* the Escalante. Looking at the map of the Dominguez-Escalante Expedition, we can easily see that the closest they got to what is now the town of Escalante was less than a hundred miles away at the place they found to ford the Colorado River, now known as the Crossing of the Fathers.

In the hundred years between the Escalante and the Powell expeditions, it is thought that Kit Carson, Jim Bridger, or government surveyor John C. Frémont *may* have explored the region. For certain, though, in June 1872 a group of men led by Powell's brother-in-law, Almon Thompson, on their way from Kanab to find a boat that had been abandoned at the mouth of the Dirty Devil, discovered a different river.

> From the mouth of the canon Potato Valley Creek flows east, say 10 miles in a straight line, then turns 40 east of south to the Colorado at a point thought to be a little above the mouth of the San Juan. It drains the east slope of Wasatch (Boulder Mountain), and the country from the cliffs south of valley . . . to within ten miles west of the Dirty Devil Mountains (Henry Mountains). It is not the Dirty Devil.

It's not clear when the river was actually named. Later, in his report, which Powell quotes in his classic *The Exploration of the Colorado River and Its Tributaries*, Thompson writes,

No animal without wings could cross the deep gulches in the sandstone basin at our feet. The stream which we had followed and whose course soon became lost in the multitude of chasms before us was not the one we were in search of but an unknown, unnamed river draining the eastern slope of the Aquarius Plateau and flowing through a deep, narrow canyon to the Colorado River. Believing our part to be the discoverers, we decided to call this stream in honor of Father Escalante, the old Spanish explorer, Escalante River and the country which it drains, Escalante Basin.

It was on Thompson's next trip to the region in 1875, when according to his journal, he met Mormons from Panguitch who were talking about making a settlement in what was then known as Potato Valley, so named because someone once found wild potatoes there. Thompson "advised them to call the place Escalante."

In his history of the region, retired Brigham Young University professor Jerry Roundy wonders whether Thompson told the Mormons that earlier, he'd named the river flowing through the valley in honor of the Catholic priest and explorer. Roundy, a dedicated Mormon, believes that "it is somewhat inaccurate to say that the town was named in honor of Father Escalante himself" but after the river and the valley, and that "it is unlikely that a group of Mormon pioneers would choose to name their town after a Catholic priest. . . . Whatever the case," Roundy believes, "the name Escalante has a certain ring to it."

I AM WRITING THIS BOOK as my response to what I have perceived as the challenge set forth in the Management Plan written for the Grand Staircase–Escalante National Monument—the Overall Vision, the second part, which says,

> the Monument provides an unparalleled opportunity for the study of scientific and historical resources. . . . The setting allows study of such important issues as: understanding ecological and climatic change over time; *increasing our understanding of the interactions between humans and their environment;* improving land management practices; and achieving a properly functioning, healthy, and biologically diverse landscape.

I can't be sure, but although the "setting allows study of such important issues," I've not heard much about how or if our "understanding of the interactions" we humans have with our environment has increased.

I doubt that this is what the plan had in mind, but my goal here is to articulate some of what the Escalante has taught me about personal wildness, about what being human really means, now and always. I want to share how the Escalante has helped me personally understand "the interactions between humans and their environment." Because the Escalante—its color, its water and rock, its original landscape, the way different light hits it in different seasons—is where the wildest remaining parts of my own body feel they've come home.

March 2004, Grassy Mesa

From the top of this mesa, I see what spring has done to this desert. I am near Boulder, Utah. It is morning. The early light is orange and the cottonwoods are smoky green with first hint of leaves. Most of the watershed drained by the Escalante River spreads out in front of me. Directly below, white Navajo sandstone domes rise up, their walls dividing green pastures where horses and cattle graze. Beyond that, the entire distance is solid—rock dunes and buttes and endless plateaus bending with the curve of the earth. Everything nonessential is gone, carried away. What's left, exposed here as nowhere else, is the earth's structure and foundation, the single basic beauty that supports all other beauty.

This was the last part of America to be explored, but there is still much left to discover. I'm surrounded by the area proclaimed by President Bill Clinton on September 18, 1996, to be the Grand Staircase–Escalante National Monument. I was here many times before that and have been here many times since.

The Grand Staircase–Escalante National Monument is divided into three sections. The westernmost is the Grand Staircase, a geological term that describes steps that climb six thousand feet in the 150 miles between the North Rim of the Grand Canyon and the Paunsaugunt Plateau in southern Utah. Each "stair" is a 2,000-foot cliff topped by a 15-mile-wide plateau. In order, beginning at the North Rim, the steps are the Chocolate, Vermillion, White, Gray, Straight, and Pink Cliffs. "It is the most colorful exposed geologic section in the world," a geology textbook proclaims, and indeed geologist Clarence Dutton is often given credit for this name.

The middle Kaiparowits Section is named for the Kaiparowits Plateau, which is also called Fifty Mile Mountain. The 1650-square-mile area includes this huge wedge-shaped block of rugged mesa and deep canyons. It may be the wildest and least known part of the monument.

The easternmost Escalante Canyons section includes the Escalante River, which winds for 1,000 miles between its beginnings on the Aquarius Plateau and Lake Powell where it ends, and the thousands of tributaries and side canyons that make this section popular with hikers and backpackers.

I will not say the real name of this mesa. I know of people who will cast spells on anyone who would accurately name places in our writing or in captions to our photographs. Those people scare me. They believe that publicizing a wild place will ultimately lead to its destruction. I guess this is possible, and although I have no personal knowledge of this occurring, I have heard stories I'm told are true. But this is not *my* reason for not naming this mesa, because I am not arrogant enough to think that my writing about this place will bring people here in sufficient numbers to destroy it. I will not name it, but only out of complete respect for you, the reader. That day in the future when you come here, having found yourself no longer in need of guidebook or map, but fueled by confidence and some deep internal force that makes you want to disappear, stretch beyond the limits of your known world, this mesa will be new. If all of us who visit this place before you take special care, your body may make you feel as if you are the first modern human to discover it, to set foot on this mesa, although your mind will know better. In this case, the feeling in your body will be stronger than the thought in your mind. I know because I have felt like the first in many places within the broad circle of which Boulder is the center, and I have known better. Knowing better has never mattered here, in this region called the Escalante.

I wonder about myself. I wonder about now and how this mesa top looks—the reddish dirt, the brilliant green of juniper and piñon, the rocky ledges, the womblike forms cut by the wind—compared to how it looked to those people who lived up here a thousand years ago. I wonder about what they saw or heard or smelled here that I, in all my modernity, am missing.

Bighorn sheep petroglyph

What I love about this place—what I love about all wild places—is how it taps some deep, old drum, how it cuts through all thought and shocks some old, elemental part of my self. I breathe in rich, aged air deep beyond the bottom of my lungs to a place where my memory is no longer mine alone but that of all of us, now and forever back and forward, that place inside me that knows how all of our earliest unnamed ancestors must have felt at that primal instant of discovery.

I climb a gradual slope between and over dark round boulders, and reach a vertical sandstone layer turned gold by the rising sun. It is a short climb and I know the route to my right and in half a minute I'm in sight of the top. The world above the vertical sandstone is different from that below it. On top, the grasses are high and clumped and I can only imagine that this place has not changed much in thousands of years. Below, the Russian thistle and cheat grass suggest overgrazing by the cows responsible for some of this county's current economy and most of its identity.

I climb a four-foot ledge and I am in a forest that without this day, this moment, I might only know from fairytales: brilliant green juniper crowns supported by trunks twisted into the faces of old women who move when I turn away.

It was here in the Escalante that I first began to believe that reality might exist in different layers, like the cliffs—layers of different sands and seas, different eons stacked on top of each other—the canyons, cross sections exposing the most recent geological events that covered the earth. Here, from this cliff, a few of the layers of reality—coverings—are visible. I can see the cultural layer off to the west—ranch buildings and plowed fields, fences and roads. This is the thinnest, yet most obvious layer. It lies on top of the layer of history, from which this current culture grew but cannot completely cover. Old barns and paths through the desert that were once wagon roads are the clues. Off the other side is the wild layer, the reality of this place before the first white settlers began to modify it. The layer of human prehistory and possibility is woven like bright thread through the wild. Here, as in very few places on earth, this thread often surfaces. Stacked stone walls in high alcoves, rock art, lithics, and pottery shards are everywhere in this country, and without a thought I catch myself scanning the rocky ledge in front of me for what might be an ancient granary.

These are the visible layers in all their richness. But there are other layers, nearly always invisible, at times heartbreaking or frustrating, and sometimes with luck and work, rewarding. The political layer will not be ignored. The federal government, under whose jurisdiction much of this land falls, is responsible for the quality of these lands and is the force against which most locals feel the need to push. The global market layer might be the strongest force, the reason parts of the local economies have failed (local ranchers and loggers are now at the mercy of multinational companies) and others have succeeded (tourists, worldwide finding their way here to see and experience the real earth, parts of it laid bare and glorious).

One other reality, another layer, is "self"—the personal dimension, my own elemental condition I've found no better way to know than being here.

That reality is layered is the only way I can understand the continual

Horses at pasture

conflicts over which of these lands should be preserved in what's left of their wild state and which should be developed for the needs of a culture that is out of control. I have been to countless meetings to discuss this issue only to come away thinking that the two sides will never agree because they refuse to understand each other, as if different languages are being spoken. I've felt it was my job to interpret the needs and desires of each side to the other, but have failed. Seeing reality layered makes my failing easier to accept. I realize that I have worked at each of the levels in an effort to see to it that these lands stay wild. I'm now working at the last, the deepest level—the self—and so far, all I have are questions: What does it mean—pure self? Is this what I'm feeling when I'm in a wild place? Is wildness one sure way to access self? And what difference does it make? And if getting closer to discovering self is a worthy goal, then why the pain, the wound that can't seem to heal, from understanding both sides of these preservation issues and knowing that at some point, deeper and bloodier, is a place where we all agree. I don't know how to get to that place.

I pause and wait. In a moment I hear what can only be a deer—four hooves hitting the ground simultaneously, legs uncoiling, launching its entire weight weightlessly and silently through the forest. Another loud contact with the ground and as I turn and catch sight of the young buck in midair our eyes meet. In a moment that time will not measure—it cannot—we are joined by this situation into one shared place, and that place will not be named. It cannot. It is only after the deer has bounded off that I can consider what has happened: at some deep cellular moment we, the deer and I, are the same, now, but back through time when we, all of us with fur, with offspring we cared for, with warm blood, were one.

I angle toward the cliff's edge to look at the view. I step off the sandy soil onto the hard light sandstone forming the cliff cap. Below me, in the dirt between my legs, I see flecks of colored stones—red and purple and dark brown, shiny black and some nearly clear enough to see through. I know that long ago an expert craftsman picked this same spot to sit, watching the view while turning rough chert into stone scrapers, knives, and atlatl points. I pick up a dark red piece. The small scallops at one edge tell me that long ago, someone had begun shaping it, perhaps with the tip of a deer antler. It is opaque and so smooth that it looks wet, and I feel as if I am holding a small, ancient organ that long ago was plucked from my own body.

Spring Break 1973, Stevens Canyon

It's meant a few flashes of almost unbearable beauty which I can only call religious experiences (and if religion means anything, that's what they were). "Fitness," and experience are part of it, too. Most important is an imperishable attitude, a philosophy if you like, a way of laying out the world and planting ourselves in it. Now we know what is trivia and what is not.

—*On the Loose*

For years before my first trip, I'd had pictures in my mind from *On the Loose*—that first small Sierra Club book, published in 1967. It was written and photographed and designed by Terry and Renny Russell—two young brothers as they wandered around what was left of the Wild West in the early sixties.

The caption in the back of the book located the photographs in "Stevens Canyon, off the Escalante River, July, 1964." The pictures seem to have been taken with an ancient camera. For years I wondered if the photographer missed the exposure or if that canyon was really that deep and dark and purple. I gave my original copy away to a nephew who I thought it might affect in the same way it affected me. To this day, my wife and I buy copies to give away whenever we come across them in used bookstores. We've kept one copy, sent to us by a photographer we met years ago while hiking near Boulder. I love what he wrote in the front:

> *I found this book in our library when I was in the 11th grade. I carried it with me everywhere and opened it when I needed to feel connected with the land and couldn't get out into the wilderness right then. I'm giving it to you because it's a book you'd understand and I kept thinking of this book while we were with you in Utah.*

Someday there should be a conference for all those people who as youngsters were inspired by that book.

I thought about those pictures the first time I set off to go backpacking in the Escalante.

I didn't have a clue what I was in for, that Friday afternoon when four of us cut classes and headed south. It was 1973 and getting to Boulder and the canyon where we wanted to hike took seven hours. (Down Interstate 15 nearly to Cedar City, over the mountains to Highway 89, south to Panguitch, east past Bryce Canyon National Park, through Tropic and the Blues to Escalante, east across the plains dropping into and out of the Escalante River, along the Hogsback, and then down into Boulder. Paving Highway 12 over Boulder Mountain in the mid-1980s cut our travel time in half.)

Dan Judd, one of my oldest friends, had been to the Escalante before. Jimmy Bradley had been on National Outdoor Leadership School courses and knew all about living in the wilderness. Shauna Smoot was a woman we all loved, but she married Jimmy a few years later. (I'm convinced that trip had something to do with it.) Although I'd been backpacking all through college, most of my trips were in the Wasatch and Uinta Mountains near Salt Lake City. I'd only recently fallen in love with desert. I had spent the previous two months on a field trip for my biology major, observing wildflowers in Death Valley, Anza Borrego, Joshua Tree, and Organ Pipe. My expectations kept me wired as we drove late into the night.

We, the last of all, are the first of all.
The oldest is always the newest,
I see nothing which I have seen before;
A man is never lost, he has only been mislaid.
Got to move, got to travel, walk away my blues.

— *On the Loose*

I RECALL that we talked about *On the Loose* during that long, first drive. We also talked about *Desert Solitaire*, Edward Abbey's classic. I think it was Jimmy who mentioned Abbey's reference to Everett Ruess. It was the first time I'd heard of this young man who escaped from California to this part of the world to write and draw and eventually disappear for completely unknown reasons. Later, I looked up what Abbey wrote about Everett Ruess. "Once caught by this golden lure you become a prospector for life, condemned, doomed, exalted. One begins to understand why Everett Ruess kept going deeper and deeper into the canyon country, until one day he lost the thread of the labyrinth."

"A prospector for life, condemned, doomed, exalted." Little did I know, that first trip to the Escalante, that this is what I was about to become.

Because of a few stops, it was past dark when we finally turned down a dirt road and camped on slick rock.

The next morning when I woke up I thought I was still dreaming. We'd camped in a wide area at the base of a long sandstone ridge rising gradually one hundred feet above. I followed the ridge with my eyes as it stretched into the distance where it curved and became one side of the gash in the rock where the river cut through. I could see the morning light bouncing between the walls—one side set on fire by the distant rising sun, reflecting onto the other causing a glowing from the deepest part of the spectrum. After a quick breakfast we broke camp and started walking. Because of the dozens of river crossings, I was glad to be wearing my Chuck Taylor Converse All Stars (which, in those simple days, I also wore to play basketball and to jog) and not my heavy leather hiking boots. I carried my huge Kelty frame pack filled with canned food and extra clothes, a winter-weight down sleeping bag and thick foam pad strapped outside.

Passage

I'd never felt *so inside anything* before as I did walking in that canyon. I love climbing mountains and looking out for the views, but this was different. This landscape seemed alive—deep, fresh air pushing against me as if exhaled from a giant, invisible lung. We walked in and out of the river and along the willow covered banks for a few hours. We stopped for a snack where a small stream ran clear out of a side canyon. I pulled out my Vienna sausages and dipped my Sierra cup into the stream and drank the cool water. While the others rested, I wandered into that side canyon. I don't know if it was the way the light hit them or magic, but the red of the monkeyflowers growing near the stream hit me like electricity, like a pleasant shock traveling up my spine. And along the walls of a shadowed alcove, I found miniature columbine and not only their brilliant yellow color, but their five long tails absorbed all of my attention as if I'd never experienced anything like this. In fact, I'd seen both of these flowers many times before. I'd studied them through the lens of natural selection, but that spring day in the Escalante, it was the pure beauty of monkeyflower and columbine that I learned not their Latin name or methods of pollination or seed dispersal. Is it just a coincidence, I asked myself, that I find these flowers so spectacular in color and form, when biologically, their appearance is simply a strategy to pass along their genes?

Is this another example of a matter of mind (science, survival, economics, and price) versus heart (love and beauty and core values)? If so, how have we as a people let matters of the heart become optional? How have we let our civilization diminish the importance of beauty in our lives?

We don't read much about the beauty of the Escalante in the writing of early Mormon pioneers. I have a friend living in Escalante who feels that her neighbors don't talk about the beauty of the place because it is so all-encompassing and elemental in their lives. I'm not sure I believe this. I think that seeing the beauty is difficult for those who live in this landscape where floods and drought and heat and cold have been major obstacles to making a decent living since the day the first Mormon pioneers arrived. Today, most of the locals don't have time to experience the area's scenic wonders and might not appreciate it if they did, having spent way too much time looking for lost cows, digging trucks out of the mud, or clearing boulders off of the highway after a flood. It might also have something to do with beliefs. As many Christians do, Mormons believe that God put resources on Earth for human consumption. I think that most Christians—Mormons included—don't consider beauty a resource equivalent to oil, gas, timber, or coal.

Growing up in Salt Lake City in a Mormon family, I remember learning in Sunday School that the beauty of the Earth as we know it is nothing compared to the Earth in its celestial, resurrected state of the next life. When I heard that, I'd already been on that first trip to the Escalante and other places more beautiful than I'd been able to imagine before seeing them. I remember thinking that I didn't need to gamble on waiting for a future life for anything more beautiful. I remember thinking that this Earth, now, was all I needed.

I imagine that the Escalante's first white settlers—and all subsequent generations— saw this wild country as theirs to try and tame and plant and harvest what they needed to live. The *Escalante Story,* the Mormon history of the area, makes no mention of natural beauty, only the potential for a mine, grassy fields that seemed to be waiting for their grazing animals, the streams that might be used for irrigation water. Louise Liston, a longtime Garfield County Commissioner whose family has always lived in or near Escalante, once commented to me as we both gazed out her front window toward the cliffs that form the Box and Death Hollow Wilderness, designated as part of the Forest Service Bill in the mid-1980s, "Yes, we're glad it's protected as wilderness, but we'd feel differently if there was oil up there, or if there might be good grazing for our cows."

The Mormon explorer and guide Jacob Hamlin didn't write much about beauty in his journals. I believe that might have more to do with his lack of formal education than his inability to appreciate it. Something tells me that had he been more comfortable writing he would have inspired us. He was a sensitive soul, known for never killing needlessly, a seasoned wanderer who would step around insects and do everything possible to avoid confrontations that might lead to injury or death. He was known for the excitement he exhibited when he received a new assignment to be a guide in the wilderness or to travel great distances through little-known country. According to his biography, "Each time Jacob had been called to lead an expedition, though he regretted leaving his family, he would become animated with expectancy and seemed eager to be on his way. Once during the days between receiving his assignment and beginning it, the neighbors were heard to remark, 'Brother Hamlin is certainly good-natured lately, as I was going by his place, he was whistling like a meadowlark.'"

Rainstorm, Coyote Gulch

I can only imagine what he saw during his life. He was the first white man to walk around the Grand Canyon, the first to visit Havasupai's turquoise pools. He was the first to explore many of the features of the Colorado Plateau that today attract millions of tourists. According to Pearson Corbett, who wrote an early in-depth biography of Jacob Hamblin, "Jacob never in all his journeys says anything of the remarkable country he explored." Hartt Wixom, in his later Hamblin biography, says that "in 1871, while attempting to find the Dirty Devil . . . to drop off supplies to Major John Wesley Powell [Hamblin] wrote, *Seenery in this canian is grand and Sublime.*" While Wixom writes that "the precise location which draws this single rave notice is not known today," others believe that it was the Escalante River he wandered down for fifty miles mistakenly thinking it was the Dirty Devil. Although I wish I knew what he thought of this country, I don't believe for one second that he walked fifty miles not knowing where he was. I believe that something came over him, pulling him down that unnamed river, drawn deeper by the high smooth walls and the stream lined by fresh green life, by the beauty and the mystery of the unknown. He couldn't have helped himself. If this is true I would understand.

Adventure is not in the guidebook, beauty is not on the map. Seek and ye shall find.

—*On the Loose*

We spent four nights in an alcove that first trip. Had we been more knowledgeable, we would have known that Desert Archaic people, early hunter-gatherers

STEVENS CANYON

31

had once lived in that canyon a thousand years before. During the day we explored side canyons so pristine we swore no humans had ever seen them. We lay on warm ledges watching red-tailed hawks playing on updrafts and imagined all of those who came before. We followed tracks of coyotes, ravens, small rodents. At night we cooked and ate and told stories that might have otherwise lain dormant. I was drawn in that first trip, and in many respects, I've never left, always wondering what the evening winter light is doing to that place, or if the river will run high enough to float. Or what will bloom with the recent rain. And when I'll be back there taking a long walk.

The last evening, I walked out of our alcove and stood on the cliff edge. It was dusk. I turned for a moment and looked back toward the alcove. Shauna was standing next to the large fire we had burning. She seemed to be in a trance as she stared into the flames. It seemed to be a familiar trance, the same trance that fire might have always brought on in humans. Her hands were in her pockets and she didn't move for a long time and neither did I. Her shadow started low on the wall behind her and curved up along the roof of the alcove and seemed to be looking down on her. Her shadow was not moving either. I snapped a picture which I kept for a while: Shauna in a deep human trance, her long dark ghost of a shadow hanging on the rock above, watching over her, watching over all of us.

September 18, 1996, The Gulch

The Gulch is a wide canyon, running off Boulder Mountain, beneath the Burr Trail and down to the Escalante River. I hike here a lot because it's close to Boulder Town and while there is considerable evidence of cattle grazing—erosion and prickly exotic plants like Russian thistle and cheat grass, and depending on the season, herds of voracious deer flies—the benches and cliffs feel completely wild. I also love the Gulch for its density of artifacts from the people who lived there over a thousand years ago. I once spent a week with an archaeologist in the lower Gulch. We camped near what was once a small

Coyote natural bridge

village, documenting one rock art panel. I still remember the third day of that trip, when I realized that other than time, not much separated the lives of those early people from my small group.

Today the Gulch is different. The summer light is easing off and turning the canyon golden beneath the cottonwoods. Moist Coyote Willows seem to comb my skin as if to scrape away crusty layers that might keep from fully experiencing this place. It's cooler than expected for early fall and a surprise rain has left the sand damp and the creek full and brown and the air is full of muskiness that rises from new water running over old ground. But those differences are all regular and semi-predictable. The difference I'm talking about is not in the air or the water. It's in me, like relief, like the last day of school, getting out of the army, sitting down after giving a public speech. A tension I'd grown used to is gone.

Two hours ago I was part of a group in Louise Liston's living room talking about the potential for what we call "compatible economic development"—projects and businesses not based on natural resource extraction, yet set up to provide employment in rural areas. I first met Louise in the late 1980s, and she's kept me confused ever since. She's supposed to be my arch enemy because of her anti-wilderness stance. Yet, I can't think of a woman who would make a better grandmother or friend. She has taught me many lessons, the most important of which is that the issues of what separate people are fewer than those that bind us—that we share more than we don't.

In the middle of our conversation, Louise suddenly picked up her remote control and switched on the television to the beginning of the ceremony wherein President William Jefferson Clinton would read a proclamation creating the Grand Staircase–Escalante National Monument. Louise was having a bad day. Fortunately, someone had leaked secret information about this proclamation, and it did not come as a complete surprise. At the time Louise was one of four Garfield County Commissioners, all of whom believed that their right to work the land and make a living from it should transcend the federal government's right, in effect, to condemn it by protecting it—giving it status of park or wilderness. Or national monument.

I realized that day in Louise Liston's living room watching the ceremony taking place on the South Rim of the Grand Canyon, that in this little town of Escalante and all the other towns strung out like beads along Highway 12, most everyone hated the idea. On the South Rim, everyone—the leaders of the American environmental movement, President Clinton, Robert Redford, and, according to Louise, "everyone but the Unabomber," loved it. While we watched the noon news, waiting for the president's speech, we talked about the weather, about tourists, the economy, and water. We talked about jams and jellies, and grandchildren. The room dimmed when the cameras shifted and panned the cliffs at the Grand Canyon. The mood changed.

We watched three speeches announcing the monument. Throughout, Louise and her husband Robert were much more polite than I would have been had the situation been reversed. "It could have been worse," they announced, referring to the fact that the Bureau of Land Management (BLM) would continue to oversee the nearly two million acres, and that grazing and water rights would not change. When it was over we all shook hands, and Louise and I hugged.

A few of us decided we'd worked enough and that it was time to hike. We chose the Gulch, now protected, now part of the Grand Staircase–Escalante National Monument.

I DOUBT THAT the Gulch's newly protected status has anything to do with it, but I seem to be moving smoother than usual, not an ache or pain. I lead the small group across the creek twice before veering right up through a break in the lowest cliff. I act as though I have a destination, which I don't, only a goal: to absorb as much of the new freedom of this place as possible.

It has been a long time coming, this new freedom, this protection. President Clinton took a bold step, but one that paled in comparison to what Harold Ickes, President Franklin Roosevelt's secretary of the interior, tried to do in the 1930s. Some things were the same. He got huge opposition from rural leaders, particularly stockmen and those interested in water, mineral, and power development. The difference between then and now—the land he wanted protected was measured not in acres, but in square miles. Ickes proposed that 6,968 square miles of southern Utah be designated as the Escalante National Monument. This was eight percent of the state, a tract of land extending two hundred miles between the Colorado and Arizona borders, containing what Park Service Director Arno Cammerer described as "an amazing wilderness labyrinth." Because of local protests, the Park Service reduced the area to 2,450 square miles. After years of political squabbling, the area was reduced to 550 square miles, which became Canyonlands National Park when it was signed into law in 1964.

In 1976 the Federal Land Policy and Management Act (FLPMA) directed the BLM to do a nationwide survey of public lands, assessing them for qualities listed in the 1964 Wilderness Act. Since forty percent of Utah is under the jurisdiction of the BLM, conservationists drooled over the possibility of protecting some of the most spectacular and astonishing roadless areas left in the United States. FLPMA had allowed fifteen years for the inventory. In Utah the original inventory took just two. According to reports, most of the inventory, including assessing an area's potential for "outstanding opportunities for solitude" was done by helicopter. Local BLM officials had taken it upon themselves to eliminate from any discussions about wilderness any land with the slightest hint of economic potential. The conservation community spent the early 1980s putting together their own inventory, including all the areas erroneously left out. The BLM recommended 1.9 million acres be designated wilderness, out of 3.2 million roadless acres. The Utah Wilderness Coalition found first 5.1 million acres and then 5.7. On March 19, 1989, Congressman Wayne Owens introduced a bill recommending the designation of 5.4 million acres. Wayne went on to become the chairman of the board of the Southern Utah Wilderness Alliance (SUWA). After losing a bid for the U.S. Senate, he chose to take on an easier conflict, the one between the Israelis and Palestinians in the Middle East. He died of a heart attack in 2002, walking on a beach near Tel Aviv. His original bill is reintroduced every year. In 2000, after Clinton's Interior Secretary Bruce Babbitt called for a new inventory, the acreage of land with wilderness qualities grew to 9.1 million acres. In 2005, environmentalists and red rock wilderness lovers across America waited patiently for the opportunity to push for the wilderness designation this area so completely deserves.

Utah's Republican Governor Mike Leavitt dreamed of solving this nagging issue on his watch and in the early 1990s designed a simple plan that if successful would create the equivalent of federal wilderness, but co-managed by the state. He would use the Escalante watershed as a pilot program, calling it the Canyons of the Escalante Eco-Region. I was part of a planning committee that had been meeting for a year when it came time to present our findings officially at a public hearing in Escalante. Since Louise had attended every meeting and had a strong say about the direction the plan should go, we felt secure as we climbed into the governor's plane to fly to Escalante. We showed up to a packed community center. The meeting was set up to allow comments at any time. We heard from the town drunk and from a Boulder man who was well known in the area for his government conspiracy theories. He was convinced that the wording we used to describe our plan came directly from Trilateral Commission documents. I asked Brad from the governor's office if he'd ever read those documents. Neither had I.

Not an hour into the meeting, it was clear that if anyone in the room liked the plan, they were too afraid to admit it. Finally, after one particularly impassioned criticism, Brad, who was running the meeting and getting increasingly frustrated, said to those in attendance, "You're obviously not happy about this. If you'd like we'll gather up all our papers and our briefcases, and leave."

Not a second went by before Escalante's own version of Paul Bunyan leaped to his feet and at the top of his lungs, screamed one of those questions that is not a question, "How can we make that happen?" None of us hesitated. We grabbed our papers and briefcases. We left so orderly that observers must have thought it was planned. We didn't look back to see if the building was burning or for the blue ox or the huge ax.

Somewhere, in some file cabinet, a concept paper exists, documenting the Canyons of the Escalante Eco-Region and its vision for a new way to manage public lands. That and a story or two are all that exist from that project.

In 1994, with some redistricting and the resulting loss of the lone Democrat, the Republicans held every Utah seat in the U.S. Congress. Governor Leavitt, who had not been in attendance in Escalante when his last idea unraveled, organized a series of meetings to be held across the state where Utah's entire congressional delegation would listen to those in attendance talk about wilderness. Then, if I remember it correctly, the county commissioners would use the information they got from the meetings, combine it with their own bias and philosophy, and make a recommendation to the governor about what BLM land should and should not be designated as wilderness. I was hired by the governor's office to gather information and help set up and run these meetings. As always, the environmental community felt that nothing good could come if the state and county commissioners were in control. After all was said and done and as expected, the governor's office drafted a bill recommending meager amounts of wilderness. What they didn't expect was the out-of-state support generated by the Utah Wilderness Coalition with national ad campaigns, traveling slide shows, and coverage in the national news. The story goes that one of Utah's most conservative, anti-wilderness congressman approached one of his colleagues from, let's say, Ohio to ask him to support what was known by the environmental community as the Anti-Wilderness Bill. The congressman from Ohio says, "Look, I'd like to support your bill, but I've had three hundred phone calls from my constituents who all tell me it's a bad bill. I've got to vote against it." And so it went, and the bill was defeated.

After the first set of meetings designed to gather information, I was given a list of questionable roads. County officials were again using roads as the reason to eliminate certain areas from the discussion. Environmentalists insisted that these roads didn't exist. My job was to photograph them.

The Gulch was on my list.

CROSSING THE DUNES and coyote tracks set in the sand since the recent rain, I look for a route through the next cliff band, which is obvious above and to my right. Deer have used the route to move from the high cliffs to the stream to drink water, and I make the easy climb up a natural staircase of flat rocks the wind and weather have chipped from the vertical wall.

On top I turn for a view and then look down on the Gulch. It is the same view I photographed years before during the wilderness debates. What had seemed at the time to be a barely recognizable remnant of a road seems to be gone, now completely obliterated by time and the healing powers of the desert.

Deer Creek in autumn

The desert changes things.

Today, on this day of protection, there is no sign that I am not the first modern white person to see this view, the wide, rock-walled canyon, the cottonwoods hinting at orange in the bottom. My friends catch up—all wearing beads of sweat—and we move higher to the next cliff band and follow it south. At a distinct bend in the wall, we notice a flat area with a circle of round volcanic boulders one to two feet in diameter in the middle. My first thought is to the stone circles in England and Wales where my ancestors came from. Then I realize that perhaps this circle was once a pit house now filled in with blown sand, the boulders placed to anchor the juniper beams that supported the roof. Nothing in my experience suggests this is accurate and yet for now it makes sense. According to the literature, these people are categorized as either Late Desert Archaic (200 B.C. to A.D. I), or Basketmaker (A.D. I to 500). They are associated with the seasonal use of the caves in the Gulch, shallow pit houses, lithic sites, rock art, and sophisticated baskets. The Fremont and the Anasazi people came after, living in pueblo-style villages, farming and making pottery.

We talk about what happened to those people and how drought or enemies or both might have pressured them to move.

Or, how the desert changes things. We talk about the new monument and what changes might result. We talk about people like Louise Liston, who want desperately to keep their quiet rural lifestyles, their unquestioned access to the resources of this wide country, their children and grandchildren all together and thriving in these strange, small towns.

And yet eventually the desert changes things. We eat a snack and drink water and move on down canyon and spread out, each in our own world.

In two hours, we're back at the car. In three, we're back at our motel watching the news for reports on the monument.

In a few months the planning will begin, everyone wanting their values represented. In a year, Harriet Priska, who owns a gift shop and gallery in Escalante, will be quoted as saying that increased business since monument designation has allowed her to pay off her mortgage three years early. New guide businesses selling maps and outdoor gear will begin to appear on Main Street, Escalante. A new bed and breakfast will be built and developers will begin looking for land to build an eco-lodge just like in Costa Rica.

In five years, I will be hired to find stories of how the monument changed everything. An outfitter will tell me that new regulations make business nearly impossible, but the owner of the new bed and breakfast is adding four rooms. There is not a hint of an eco-lodge. And Harriet Priska now wonders if her increased business was due to monument designation or to the fact that she started selling petrified wood.

Change comes slowly in the desert.

April 2000, The Moody Loop

Eight of us are crammed into the shade left by a red boulder the size of a small car. It is April and this year seems to have skipped spring and launched directly into summer. We are three days into a loop hike which started in Moody Canyon, where we left our cars. We have traversed dozens of other canyons that have remained unnamed due perhaps to the fact that few people have visited them for reasons that are becoming clear. For hours, we've been wandering along a high mesa top, moving through the soft sand and clumps of high grasses in the wide spaces between small junipers. We could be looking out over the Grand Staircase–Escalante National Monument, across a spectacular sunken tangle of canyons to Fifty Mile Mountain forming the horizon in the distance. But we're not. We are resting, trying to cool and heal, or dreaming of the future, which in our case is only guaranteed for the next few hours.

Biggest, short for Biggest Bob who is bigger than both Big Bob and Bob, two other hikers who frequently join this group, has pulled off the brace supporting the fifty-year-old knee he'd recently had repaired, and more recently—within the past hour—hyper-extended when a rock he stepped on collapsed beneath his two hundred-plus pounds. Ted is out—sound asleep. Kathie has her shoes off, exposing bright red feet. Steve is lost, but not exactly. I can tell by how he waves his GPS. It's when he starts banging it against his leg that I worry. I am panting while ants or sweat, I can't tell which, run down my nose. I am down to half a quart of water, which is more than I can say for the rest of the group. But no worries.

Steve says, "We'll be camping next to the most beautiful spring, surrounded by cattails, with birds and dragonflies fluttering about." He adds, "If it hasn't dried up like all the others." He chuckles.

We are here for many reasons, all but one of which have been momentarily forgotten. We are here because we are FOS's—friends of Steve's. Steve is Steve Allen, a tree-tall man with a wide smile and mischief in one eye. Steve has spent years wandering the Colorado Plateau, logging over 10,000 miles to discover the routes he has detailed in each of the three guidebooks he has written over the past decade. We have been with him before and we know with 90 percent confidence that none of us will die—better odds than Everest.

Sandstone tower

No one is talking. I am reminded while looking around the group that among us are an ex-lawyer, an ex-obstetrician, an ex-plumbing supply salesman, an ex-owner of a small high-tech company, and an ex-auto mechanic. Together, we could be running a small town, were we not plopped down in the dirt feeding our bodies to ants because we are too tired to move and too thirsty to care. I think about all the parents who want nothing more than for their children to find their way into careers promising financial security. Then I think about how financial security has become modern society's definition of survival, and how out here, that definition is about as useful as the guarantee that the manufacturer of my boots will replace them if they fall apart. Assuming I make it back alive. All of us worked hard at financial security and even while we were doing it, we knew it wasn't enough. We could feel something inside us that didn't give a whit about financial security.

Is that what we're doing out here, practicing the truest sense of survival, at least the truest sense available to Middle Americans in the twenty-first century? Maybe.

Try to imagine a time when people had four things to worry about—food, water, shelter, and safety. Nowadays, we have these worked out. Even out here in the big open, the long view, the deep unknown, we've got food (we're each carrying our own lunches and breakfast and one dinner for the whole group), we have tents (for the slim chance that we might see a cloud, let alone rain), and we're quite safe (of three desperados who killed a policeman in Colorado, two have already turned up dead, we're near no bombing ranges, and the predators still hunting here prefer antelope ground squirrels and grasshoppers).

The only thing missing is water. So, what began as a recreational loop hike, a vacation, ends in a struggle for survival? In a way. More of a drill than reality, but who cares?

What we've done for water:

Above Middle Moody, three of us climbed a steep crack to gain another level, and then dragged the others, one at a time, up a nearly vertical wall. Those potholes were dry.

The unnamed canyon with the one-inch deep pool that required two people (one to hold the other's belt while she reached down from the only stable perch, and two hours to fill six quart bottles.

The one hundred feet up and down we needed to go for every ten feet of forward along the Waterpocket Fold, so named for more than the one "waterpocket" we managed to find.

The three-man-high human ladder we needed to extricate Jimbo from the ledge in the canyon above Hall's Creek, where he sat to belay us down the vertical slickrock wall to the pools we had seen from above.

Then the shallow, muddy water we strained through Kathie's T-shirt (we voted it the cleanest).

Sure, we could have stayed home and turned on the tap, but look what we'd missed—the recreation, the vacation free from life's stress and strain. All that plus rock art and ruins, unlimited vistas, bighorn sheep (the band of six we followed along a wide sandstone ledge and the skull of a full-curl ram), birds

Waterfall

(raptors, fly-catchers, and a lazuli bunting, for example), and nights under blankets of stars. The list of all the reasons we want to go backpacking is different from the list of reasons why we *need* to go backpacking.

Wanting to go backpacking has to do with personal preference. *Needing* to go backpacking goes beyond that to a global and possibly human scale. I've made a hobby of studying why modern humans need to go backpacking. The research has been time-consuming and rewarding. I've done it, not to rationalize my behavior, although this is something of which I'm often accused, but to make some sense of my life. It may be that I'm nearing fifty, but I need to see myself in a larger frame of reference than here and now.

This is good to think about now; as we're all quiet in the shade, and I'm surely opened up to the gnawing questions about why we didn't stay home and take the family to Disney World. At first I think about engaging the group in conversation, but then I look around and think again. No one wants to hear why I think we all need to be here. I know, however, that I'll feel better if I let my mind wander back through my research.

Paul Shepard was the writer who planted the seed in me suggesting that since the human body has not changed much in the past hundred thousand years, we will probably respond in the same way to some of the same stimuli that played key roles in the lives of our primitive ancestors. I interpret that to mean anything wild—everything that has escaped our modern influence. He said that "civilization is a veneer" and beneath that veneer is a basic human core that is programmed to function in a world vastly different from the one we're currently living in. So, what is in that core? What kept us going over the course of all those eons we were busy getting to who we are now?

In her poem "Yes, No!" Mary Oliver writes, "Imagination is better than a sharp instrument," which is important in thinking about getting into that core.

I think that Bernard G. Campbell managed a peek inside that core in his book, *Human Evolution*. He wrote about four characteristics that have contributed to our success as a species. He calls them the Four Evolutionary Novelties. Humans maintain a constant body temperature, making life possible in different climates and seasons. With different kinds of teeth—incisors to tear with, molars to grind with—they can eat many different kinds of food. Female humans give birth to young that are at an advanced stage of development and survival is more likely. The Fourth Novelty is the exploratory drive, the *need* to explore and learn from our environment. He writes, "The exploratory drive is a behavioral development, which by making possible better knowledge of the environment increases the chances for survival of the individual, and therefore the species."

My body temperature is constantly at 98.6 (today it might argue). I have different teeth to tear meat, munch carrots, and crush bread. I was born fairly complete. This week, with my friends, I am exploring the environment. I'll take for granted that my survival is more likely because I'm here wandering through this desert. And it is not just about finding water. The Four Novelties that have insured the survival of our species from the get-go apply to me, here, now. I have to trust that being here in the wilderness is also good for the species, just as it has been for an awfully long time.

It seems to me that something has short-circuited. Humans still use that Fourth Novelty, but mainly in learning how to make individual lives longer. Somehow the *survival of the individual* has become detrimental to the long-term survival of our species. Somehow we've come to accept that someone is alive if he breathes, if his heart beats, even if that heart once belonged to someone else.

In my imagination, life is a broad river flowing from the past into the future, full of every living thing, all interacting. Somehow, we've been arrogant enough to think we can step out of that river, letting it flow by. We watch it and reach in to grab what we need or want, never moving, as if somehow we know we're in the right place. We have stepped out of life's real river. Backpacking is stepping back in.

If water had been the only reason to hike in the Escalante for a week, then we would have been better off staying next to the trucks, each of which stored five-gallon jugs full of it. Or better still, we would have stayed home where we could unconsciously walk to the sink on our way to the refrigerator. But look what we'd have missed. While I've never been able to describe why backpacking is important to me, phrases like "outdoor recreation" and "active vacation" never come close. Now I understand. Backpacking is one way we explore. From the beginning, exploration has been necessary for our survival. Maybe it still is. I'll keep doing my part. I'll keep going beyond the edge of this known, broken world, into the little known, the unknown, the Escalante, and coming back with water and stories of what I've seen. Just like always.

April 2003, Calf Creek

Eight of us assemble in the Calf Creek picnic area. We've been attending a meeting at the Boulder Mountain Lodge up the road, and this is free time until dinner and more meetings. This is hiking time and I'm the guide. Lower Calf Creek, from the falls to the Escalante River, may be the least-wild and most emblematic canyon in the entire drainage. The entrance and parking area are paved. A modern kiosk has information developed for the masses—people who might not already know to take water and wear sturdy shoes. You pay to park and for a published trail guide to numbered posts set at points of interest along the way.

I have been to Lower Calf Creek more than anywhere in all of southern Utah. It feels very familiar. I have walked the 2.75 miles to Calf Creek Falls dozens of times: carrying children, holding the hands of old people, running for exercise after stressful meetings. Once, I helped set up a Jewish wedding at Calf Creek Falls, complete with the awning and little caps.

I have been there in every season: when the heat from the sand forced its way through my shoes and when frigid air froze creek water into thick strands as it seeped through beaver dams. I have seen cottonwoods in every shade of green, in gold, in black and white. Today is clear and warm, the sky an infinite blue dome.

Recently, some things began occurring to me. Maybe it is because I am getting older and perhaps more conservative that I no longer feel driven to exploration, to finding new routes in unknown places. Maybe I'm rationalizing my personal taming or in denial, but I'm finding deep meaning in getting to know Calf Creek in the way that is not possible without visiting it over and over. In fact, after frequent visits to this place, I feel closer to understanding *place* as a concept, a human factor, as elemental.

I suggested Calf Creek to the group because during the three or four hours it takes to walk to the falls and back, we'll sample everything that sets the wild world of the Escalante apart from the modern world—I knew from experience that half a dozen flowers will be blooming, that small trout will dart between shadows at two points where the trail and stream nearly intersect. We will see remnants of an old fence built to contain the calves owned by the earliest Mormon settlers a hundred years ago. One thousand years ago, "Long Time

Calf Creek falls

Ago People"—Fremont and the ancient ancestors of the Puebloans—built a granary to store corn they grew. We'll stop to find that high on one far wall. On another we will see three towering red figures painted. If we are willing to pay the attention required, we will see more than a dozen bird species: besides ravens and robins, perhaps towhees, pinion jays, and chickadees. If luck is with us we'll see a pair of ouzels perched on the wet alcove wall picking at the insects attached there. Or a peregrine falcon that we will only know by its small size and huge speed. Only if one of us is cursed will we *not* hear the cascading notes of the canyon wren.

I did not mention three things to the group: that I believe that groups of people should go to places that are managed for groups of people; that I consider this place to be a pilgrimage of sorts; and at the end of the trail is a place where all of the water in this world drops over the edge of the cliff and crashes into a pond where a man once caught a huge brown trout using a gopher for bait. Or so I've heard.

Before we've walked a quarter mile, the group is spread out in twos and threes. Four of us have stayed back. I'm busy touching and naming things—I can't help myself. I'm excited to see the huge cliffrose in full bloom. Off to the left, three feet from the trail, something catches my eye. The sun's perfect angle hits an irregular piece of stone. It is a beautiful piece of red chert chipped from the edge of a knife or point. Either ten thousand people have walked by this without noticing or it was just moved here by the water from recent rain.

We catch up with some of the others at the post marking the pictographs at the base of the alcove across the canyon. These tall figures with their red-horned headdresses, their arms and legs, are thought to be Fremont. Of all that the Escalante canyons offer, it's the connection to the past through the archaeological remnants I find here that attracts me the most. What did they know by living out their entire lives in places like this? What did they believe and how did they explain the world? What does this art say about their lives?

I pass my binoculars around the group so everyone can see the rock art figures in more detail. We wonder out loud what they mean, and one person draws the figures in her notebook. In five minutes they are gone and I am alone with my binoculars. I scan the three figures over and over and then move my vision above and below them and to both sides. I suddenly realize that what I'd thought for years was wrong—that the markings on the wall below and left of the three red figures were irregularities in the sandstone. It is actually more rock art, layer upon layer of petroglyphs, like remnants of an ancient conversation between artists passing by this way.

I think back to an article I read recently by Amos Rapoport, an Australian architect whose own curiosity about place and its meaning in our modern lives led him to study the mythical landscapes of Aboriginal people. There are still groups of Australian Aborigines on whom the modern world has had little effect, and Rapoport thought that understanding their relationship to their place might contribute to our knowing place as an elemental yet forgotten part of our lives. Rapoport knew that the stories by which members

ESCALANTE

58

of Aboriginal tribes know their origin, their purpose, and their meaning are grounded in the landscape, in place. The myths are just myths until the land makes them real. Without their land, the people cannot be real.

The land makes people real. What does that say about us? I've spent most of my life thinking about the Escalante and other wild places I've seen and come to care about. But I've never considered how places—especially wild places—make us real or how they might help us to know our true meaning and purpose in the universe. To many critics of America, we don't seem real, but rather programmed working robots designed to build and consume products of a young technological culture that has no depth and no story. And if meaning and purpose in the universe seem to be lacking in modern America as many would argue, might the cause have something to do with the fact that we've cut ourselves off from *place* in our lives?

To Aborigines and all "primitive" people, being native goes well beyond living in place and getting to know everything about it. Being native has attached to it dimensions of time and generations of ancestors who have all lived in the same place and given enough deep, old meaning to it to make it sacred. Can we become native to a place? Can a place be truly sacred to us, now that we've cut ourselves off from most of our ancestors? I don't know. According to Rapoport, when Aborigines move through their country they are linking two worlds, the mythical with the physical. They become the link. "Aborigines do not move just in a landscape, but in a humanized realm saturated with significations." In this realm, physical features have a larger

ESCALANTE

60

meaning that has been passed down by story and song through four hundred generations. It is as if particular rocks, for example, have absorbed the stories and songs and give them off, radiate them when someone with knowledge passes by. Signals.

Four hundred generations. I think about that in context, in Calf Creek where yes, different rocks and trees and high walls remind me of when I've been here before. But four hundred generations of meaning and purpose in the universe, four hundred generations in one place. How do we replace that? We don't. We can't. We can start now, saving places like Calf Creek, and coming back over and over, each time with more meaning to leave for the next people passing through.

I find half of the group moving slowly along the last stretch of trail. Everyone is quiet as if the strength of the silence is pressing in against them. One last bend and falling water can be heard in the distance, and then felt in the fresh breeze formed when the falling water forces the air down canyon. The idea of moving water energizes us and we pick up our pace. And then, there it is, no longer a surprise but a gift and we all stand and watch as if seeing water fall for the first time, between red canyon walls turned green with moss and maidenhair fern. In a moment our ears adjust and the roar of the water falling 126 feet becomes its own basis for silence.

We eat lunch and wander around to see the effect of all this water on a desert. Then we begin our walk back. In less than a mile, I find a woman, not from our group, on her way in. She has stopped dead in her tracks. At first I think she must see something, but when I look in the direction she's staring,

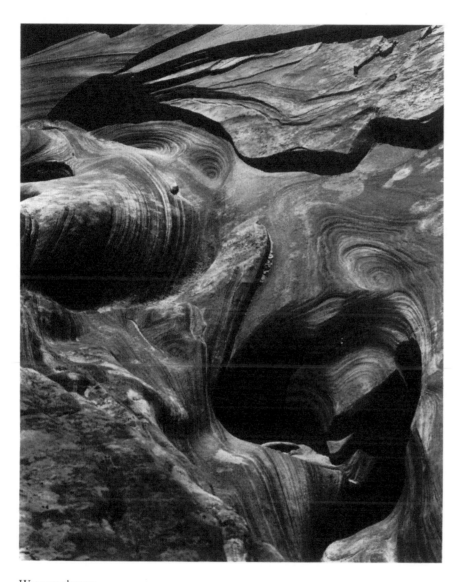

Water sculpture

I don't see anything. Then I notice. A breeze has shifted and caught in it the scent of desert holly, the yellow flowers of Fremont's mahonia. I have read about this intoxication, but never until now experienced it. I have a difficult time imagining something so invisible having so much power.

For a moment I, too, am paralyzed.

May 2004, Big Horn

The guidebook says the hike we want to take tomorrow begins two miles from the turnoff. We've traveled 8.4 and now we're pulled off onto the one area we've seen that is flat enough to keep me from sliding around in the back of my truck later when I try to sleep. I make a mental note of the answer to the math problem of what my odometer will need to read when we stop after backtracking in the morning. Chris Noble is setting up his tent. Chris and I have been best friends for twenty years. His passion for capturing the essence of wildness with his camera is matched only by his search for meaning in this modern world that does its best to commodify and dilute it.

With the clouds, it is hard to tell how soon the sun will drop out of sight.

With no tent to set up I spend my time gathering round, metal-like stones. On the surface of certain random outcroppings they have rolled and gathered like marbles in every low point. I have seen them before and wondered where they came from and why. One possibility: An exploding volcano, distant in both time and space, spewed near-vaporized lava bubbles so high in the air that by the time they reached the ground they had cooled and turned to stone. Whether this is true or not, it is the story I tell when I give one to someone who needs to hold perfection in her hand.

The cooler becomes the table and the tailgate holds the stove and we sit in lawn chairs, letting the silence suck out all we carried here that could possibly confuse us. I have spent most of my life trying to make sense of why moments like this work for me and why the language of our culture cannot seem to accommodate simplicity this pure. Rio has no trouble making sense of this. Rio is the African Basenji who lives with me, who never questions whether wild remnants are still active inside him and neither do I. He spends his time hunting or as a bright brown puddle in the sand, just as his relatives in Africa have done since before the pharaohs.

We are parked in the middle of what the map refers to as the Escalante Canyons Section of the Grand Staircase–Escalante National Monument. If I'd not spent dozens of hours reading maps and days driving these roads and hiking here, I might wonder, like many who were outspoken against any federal

Approaching storm, Strike Valley

designation of this area, what is so special about this place. From where we sit there are no canyons, only rocky outcroppings separated and surrounded by pink sand where wind-bent junipers grow with dozens of wildflower species, and rich, dark organic crusts struggle to survive the trampling of cattle. The road we came in on is typical of many in this monument—smooth enough for most vehicles, stretching across some of the least civilized places left in America—the "high lonesome." For many, it is enough to be in space this big and this old. But it is not all there is. We know from experience that out of sight, beyond the end of every road, is a long, hard edge, still being broken and cut as the canyons for which this place is famous, eat it away.

Tonight, we eat whatever we have that can be cooked in boiling water, and we drink beer, and a conversation that would be difficult in a different setting drops out of us like rocks from cliffs—about women, the power of dreams, and what gives meaning to our lives and what takes it away. New ideas form here as if from seeds that have found their first fertile place to grow. I have learned to question the quality, the importance, or the truth of ideas coming from anywhere else.

Talking into the night, we sense that if we stop for too long, silence may fill in the spaces our words leave with such weight and force to keep us paralyzed in our chairs until the morning birdsong builds enough to break it. Finally, I realize I can no longer fight, I use the last of my strength to stand and move slowly to my bed. Rio is already there, fast asleep on my pile jacket.

The morning comes in an instant—one second everything washed in predawn purple, and the next exploding in bright orange as the sun clears the distant cliff. I am surprised that somehow Chris has managed to overcome the weight of last night's silence and has wandered off looking for a photograph. He's back by the time the water boils, and we eat and pack. In no time, we're turned around and driving toward the trailhead.

All my calculations add up, and in fifteen minutes we pull off the road into a space big enough to park out of traffic, although we have not seen another vehicle since we left the pavement. We believe that we are in the right place because a footpath appears the moment we step away from the truck.

There are no fresh tracks, only compressed soil and an eighteen-inch-wide absence of growth to indicate that we are not the first humans to explore this corner of the Earth. My first thought is to curse the guidebook, because without it, there would be no path and I might believe I was discovering this place. My second thought is to catch my first thought and keep it from gaining momentum and to remember that without the guidebook we would not be here. I look south into the direction we're headed. From where I stand, there is no indication that this is the beginning of an amazing day.

Steve Allen wrote the guidebook we're using, as well as two others. He has been both criticized and praised for them. He is a friend, and when we talk about guidebooks, we don't argue because he believes that people who use his guidebooks to find impossible wild places are likely to become advocates for saving them. He believes this because this is what happened to him. During the years he spent walking ten thousand miles to find the places he chose to include in his books, he became one of the most ardent supporters of wilderness designation, and today spends his own time and money traveling the country showing slides of what is at stake. In the end, if the wild parts of the West remain protected for the future, it will be due to the combined voices of many people speaking up—not only about the importance of wildness to modern society, but also about whom they have become because of the time they spent there.

In half an hour, we arrive at that edge, the top of a canyon, the hard line separating this world from that, and drop in.

Rio is out ahead of us. I can see his fresh tracks, but no sign of him. The sun is direct and sprays down light that bounces side to side, coating the smooth canyon walls in rich yellow-orange. I pretend we are exploring inside a gigantic fruit—a peach or mango. The sand is deep and a bit difficult to walk in. Besides Rio's, the two-day-old coyote route, a large stinkbug's zippered path, and leaf-like raven imprints, ours are the only tracks.

It is simple to think that finding a place within a national monument as beautiful as this and discovering we have it all to ourselves must be due to the fairly recent designation and the fact that plans for marked trails and signage (the closest monument sign is miles away) have not yet been implemented.

The walls darken and the canyon deepens the further into it we go. In places, it narrows down and we must take off our packs and turn sideways to pass. Then the canyon walls spread and smooth, our stride lengthens in the sand, and our attention softens. We round a bend and immediately the sand turns to stone which splits open, exposing a chasm of smooth twisting rock, dark enough and deep enough to challenge infinity. Twice this happens and we need to find a high route around it.

Finding our way. This must be our highest human calling. The guidebook

Labyrinth

brought us here, told us where this canyon begins and ends and some ideas of what to expect.

Finding our way. Finding our own way. Our own way is not in the guidebook.

We have found our deep rhythm and realize that it is not something we've consciously been looking for, but it is very real and we only know it when we feel it. This rhythm, this bonelike feeling might actually be a memory we can only have when our bodies remember the truth of what being human means. What if this can only happen once we've discovered that basic deep 100,000-year-old part in us that cannot be changed, only covered by layers of a civilization that now seems headed for its own destruction? And what if we can only begin to understand it in the presence of an uncovered, complete, and wild landscape? And what if we expose this old, human part of us, the part responsible for changing and adapting and ultimately for the very success of our species, and find that it still works?

Our improvised route takes us up a rubble-strewn crack. Rio disappears beneath boulders, and we don't see him again until we reach a wide, level layer where we find him sitting, waiting. It takes just a few minutes to pass the deep obstacle, and fifty feet below us the canyon bottom is flat and sandy again, beckoning us down. Without thinking we abandon the higher, more direct route, choosing instead the deeper, inner path. We know from the guidebook that this hike can easily be done in one day. We also know that whether this is a long or a short day depends on how quickly we move and how many detours we take. Back in the streambed, we unconsciously choose a long day. Instead of turning down stream toward our goal, we turn up stream to explore the deep twisting rock we'd found our way around. It is a short section. Within ten feet the walls are too close to get between and we move further only by climbing up eight feet and shinnying along with our feet on one wall pressing our backs against the other. Rio continues along below us, pulling his twenty-five-pound body between the walls. I hope that he is too smart to get stuck because I'm not sure how I would help him. The canyon widens in twenty feet, forming a space big enough to stand and look up the vertical fall to a small sliver of blue sky and wonder how we might save ourselves if the world behind us suddenly closed in around us. Rio has better sense and without room enough to turn around is backing out the way he came. So far, I've found that there is always a way out of the desert.

I've spent years trying to find the words to explain this connection I feel between the inner and outer landscapes. Last year, I found a book at a library sale, C. A. Meier's *The Soul and the Body: Essays on the Theories of Carl Jung*. I bought the book after reading in the table of contents that one of the essays was titled, "Wilderness and the Search for the Soul of Modern Man," which is from a speech Meier gave in 1983.

According to Meier, early philosophers believed that "man was a small cosmos containing everything in the world, that true understanding and perception is only possible by an outpouring of the macro-cosmos (outer nature) into the micro-cosmos (our own inner natures or souls)." Meier believes that "the wilderness inside would really go wild if we should badly damage the outer wilderness. So, let's keep the balance the best we can in order to maintain sanity." Insanity, as I understand it, is being out of touch with the unconscious, which is a key component of the self, which many believe is made up of the soul.

I'm thinking about what Meier wrote while Chris consults the guidebook to determine if the wide canyon coming in on our left is the beginning of our route back. Although high clouds filter the midday sun, the air is hot and feels good and my limbs feel loose and light. We follow a game trail that cuts off a long meander in the streambed, which takes us up a small rise through a field so thick with primrose that we need to watch our step to avoid smashing them. A nearly straight line marks the top of the rise, where the white carpet of primrose turns bright orange with globe mallow. Rio takes advantage of even the smallest shade—a thick rabbitbrush or sage, a tiny alcove formed when a flood undermined a soft sandstone wall. Meier, by suggesting that a balance between the inner and outer wilderness is the key to sanity, provides what might be the best argument yet for preserving these places, and possibly the perfect explanation for our current state of affairs.

We know we're on the right route when the wide pale canyon pinches off into a purple wound-like gash. We leave our packs, knowing that there is no way out. We are drawn in by the nearly magnetic force of these unique walls, which seem to have been embossed with perfect parallel lines, and I think this might be the most beautiful place I've ever seen. We run our hands along the walls, and when we talk the sound of our voices barely overcomes the silence.

After backtracking, we climb a long sandstone ridge. From here the guidebook merely points us in the right direction, and we begin an overland route that will take us up over domed plateaus, in and out of nameless washes, between endless pink sand dunes. We stop only for water and to pick up and turn around in our hands a chert scraper once used for creating fiber from yucca and a broken arrowhead lying on bedrock as if dropped yesterday. We walk and walk across miles of open country. Somewhere invisible in the distance we will come to the road we drove in on. Although we are tired, we move smoothly. Once again, I am amazed at how easily, in the Escalante, my body remembers how to be human.

notes

INTRODUCTION

Silvestre Velez Escalante, *The Dominguez-Escalante Journal: Their Expedition Through Colorado, Utah, Arizona, and New Mexico in 1776,* ed. Ted J. Warner and Fray Angelico Chavez (University of Utah Press, 1995).

Jerry C. Roundy, *"Advised Them to Call the Place Escalante"* (Springville, Utah: Art City Publishing, 1998; John Wesley Powell, *The Exploration of the Colorado River and Its Canyons* (Dover, 1961).

As of 2006, copies of the Monument Plan and other information could be found at http://www.ut.blm.gov/monument/Visitor_Information/visitor_information.html or from Grand Staircase–Escalante National Monument, 180 West 300 North, Kanab, Utah 84741.

For information on the area's prehistoric cultures, see Duncan Metcalf's archaeology chapter in *Visions of the Grand Staircase-Escalante,* edited by Robert B. Keiter, Sarah B. George, and Joro Walker (Utah Museum of Natural History, 1998).

SPRING BREAK 1973, STEVENS CANYON

Terry and Renny Russell, *On the Loose* (Sierra Club Books, 1967; reprinted by Gibbs Smith, 2001).

For information on Everett Ruess, see W. L. Rusho's *Everett Ruess: Vagabond for Beauty* (Gibbs Smith, 1985); W. L. Rusho, ed., *The Wilderness Journals of Everett Ruess* (Gibbs Smith, 1998); and Gary James Bergera and Everett Ruess, *On Desert Trails with Everett Ruess* (Desert Magazine, 1950).

Pearson H. Corbett, *Jacob Hamlin, Peacemaker* (Deseret Books, 1952); Hartt Wixom, *Hamblin: A Modern Look at the Frontier Life and Legend of Jacob Hamlin* by (Cedar Fort Incorporated, 1996.)

SEPTEMBER 18, 1996, THE GULCH

As of 2006, www.suwa.org contained information on wilderness preservation and the Southern Utah Wilderness Alliance.

Elmo R. Richardson, The Escalante National Monument Controversy of 1935–1940. *Utah Historical Quarterly* 33 (Utah State Historical Society, Spring, 1965)

Harriet Priska was interviewed about her mortgage burning party in the *New York Times* (October 13, 1997).

APRIL 2000, THE MOODY LOOP

Steve Allen's guidebooks are *Canyoneering: The San Rafael Swell* (University of Utah Press, 1992); *Canyoneering 2, Technical Loop Hikes in Southern Utah* (University of Utah Press,

1994); and *Canyoneering 3: Loop Hikes in Utah's Escalante* (University of Utah Press, 1997).

Some books by Paul Shepard are *Nature and Madness, The Tender Carnivore, and the Sacred Game,* and *Man in the Landscape.* Some collections have been produced: *Traces of an Omnivore* and *The Paul Shepard Reader.*

Bernard G. Campbell, *Human Evolution: An Introduction to Man's Adaptations* (Aldine de Gruyter, 1985).

APRIL 2003, CALF CREEK

As of 2006, www.boulder-utah.com and www.hellsbackbonegrill.com contained information on the Boulder Mountain Lodge and the Hell's Backbone Grill.

As of 2006, more on the Fremont Indians written by archaeologist David Madsen could be found at http://www.onlineutah.com/fremontindianhistory.shtml

Barry Lopez wrote about Amos Rapoport in *Arctic Dreams* (Scribners, 1986). Rapoport's article "Australian Aborigines and the Definition of Place" is part of *Shelter, Sign, and Symbol,* edited by Paul Oliver (Overlook Press, 1980).

Terry Tempest Williams wrote about silence and distraction in her book *Leap* (Pantheon Books, 1996).

David Williams wrote about the "intoxicating proportions" of *Mahonia fremontii* in *A Naturalist's Guide to Canyon Country* (Falcon Press, 2000).

MAY 2004, BIG HORN

C. A. Meier, *The Soul and the Body: Essays on the Theories of Carl Jung* (Lapis Press, 1986).

about the author

Brooke Williams is a writer and consultant to businesses, local governments, and nonprofit organizations on issues of management, social entrepreneurship, and compatible economic development. For the past thirty years, Brooke has actively pursued adventure in wild landscapes and he believes in using lessons learned from nature's ability to adapt to constantly changing conditions in organizational transformation. Brooke has an MBA in Sustainable Business from the Bainbridge Graduate Institute and a Biology degree from the University of Utah. He is also the author of *Utah: A Celebration of the*

Landscape with photography by Tom Till, *Halflives: Reconciling Work and Wildness*, and many articles. *Escalante: The Best Kind of Nothing* is his second book with Chris Noble, the first being *Utah Ski Country* published in 1986 by Utah Geographic Series.

Brooke currently serves as the Executive Director of the Murie Center in Moose, Wyoming, where he's involved in discussions about a deeper, more inclusive, and more effective environmental movement. He is married to the writer Terry Tempest Williams.

about the photographer

From the slopes of Everest to the jungles of Borneo, Chris Noble has been on assignment to the ends of the earth photographing for clients including *National Geographic*, The North Face, *Outside*, Nike, and *Rolling Stone*. One of the most widely published outdoor photographers working today, his imagery has been included in hundreds of publications worldwide and in books such as *Exposure* (Outside Magazine) and *Malaysia: Heart of Southeast Asia* (Archipelago Press). *American Photo Magazine* wrote, "the secret to

Noble's success is that there is no dividing line between adventure and his photography."

Noble's recent work (www.noblefoto.com) explores the spiritual dimension of remote landscape, ancient culture and man's evolving relationship to the earth; he is now applying his vision and skill to projects that aid in the transformation to a more mindful, more compassionate, and sustainable world.

Library of Congress Cataloging-in-Publication Data

Williams, Brooke.

    Escalante : the best kind of nothing / text by Brooke Williams ;
photographs by Chris Noble.

      p. cm. – (Desert places)

    Includes bibliographical references.

    ISBN-13: 978-0-8165-2458-7 (pbk. : alk. paper)

    ISBN-10: 0-8165-2458-0 (pbk. : alk. paper)

    1. Escalante River Region (Utah)—Description and travel.
2. Williams, Brooke—Travel—Utah—Escalante River Region.
3. Escalante River Region (Utah)—Pictorial works. 4. Escalante
River Region (Utah)—History. 5. Natural history—Utah—Escalante
River Region. 6. Escalante River Region (Utah)—Environmental
conditions. I. Title. II. Series.

F832.E83W55 2006

917.92'520434—dc22

                                   2006013558